The Identity Thief

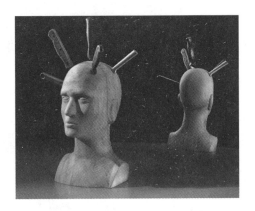

Derek Mong

Distributed by University Press of New England
Hanover and London

No part of this book may be used or reproduced in any manner without written permission except in the case of brief quotations embodied in critical articles and reviews. Please direct inquiries to:

Saturnalia Books
105 Woodside Rd.
Ardmore, PA 19003
info@saturnaliabooks.com

ISBN: 978-0-9980534-6-2
Library of Congress Control Number: 2018949140

Book Design by Robin Vuchnich
Printing by Versa Press
Cover Art: "Your Best Kitchen Mate! Knife block," designed and manufactured by Maarten Baas (German, b. 1978)

Author Photo: Anne O. Fisher

Distributed by:
University Press of New England
1 Court Street
Lebanon, NH 03766
800-421-1561

Always Crashing: "The Environmentalists"; *American Literary Review*: "Midnight at the School of Cosmetology," "Heliotrope, Or Man's Mind Angles Inevitably Toward God," and "The Second Year"; *Artful Dodge*: "In the Shadow of a Scrivener's Quill"; *Blackbird*: "Colloquy with St. Mary of Egypt"; *Blue Lyra Review*: "An Ordinary Evening in San Francisco"; *Cider Press Review*: "Lightning 2" (as "Lightning 3"); *Cincinnati Review*: "The First Heartbeat"; Colorado Review: "Litany"; *Crab Creek Review*: "Glaciers"; *The Cream City Review*: "Lightning 1" (as "Lightning 2"); *Free Verse: A Journal of Contemporary Poetry & Poetics*: "Dementia" and "Lightning 3" (as "Lightning 5"); *Hawai'i Pacific Review*: "Old Tyme with a *y*"; *The Laurel Review*: "To Assemble This Poem Properly," "We Live Our Lives through Other People's Bodies," "To Translate This Poem Properly," and "Hide and Seek"; *The Missouri Review*'s "Poem of the Week" (online): "The Air"; *Pleiades*: "The Identity Thief"; *Poetry Northwest*: "Letter in a Bottle for When the Seas Rise"; and *River and Sound Review*: "Thumbprint."

"In the Shadow of a Scrivener's Quill" and "Midnight at the School of Cosmetology" also appeared in *Redux* (online). "We Live Our Lives through Other People's Bodies" won the 2018 Wolverine Farms Broadside Competition; it also appeared in *concis: min words, max heart* (online). "Thumbprint" appeared in the "Poetry Jumps Off the Shelf" postcard series from Woodrow Hall Editions. "To Assemble This Poem Properly," "Heliotrope, Or Man's Mind Angles Inevitably Toward God," "To Translate This Poem Properly," and "The Air" appeared in *Enclave* 7 (China) with accompanying Mandarin translations by Qin Sun Shu. "An Ordinary Evening in San Francisco" also appeared in *Last Call: The Anthology of Beer, Wine, & Spirits Poetry* and *Wabash Magazine*. I am thankful to Two Sylvias Press, who published "Litany," "In the Shadow of a Scrivener's Quill," "Hide and Seek," and

"Heliotrope, Or Man's Mind Angles Inevitably Toward God" in a chapbook, *The Ego and the Empiricist*, which was a finalist for the Two Sylvias Press Chapbook Prize.

Thank you David Baker, Maggie Glover, Eleanor Goodman, H. L. Hix, Jason Koo, Deborah Landau, John Miller, D. A. Powell, Justin Tackett, and the University of Louisville's Axton Fellowship. Thank you Henry Israeli, Christopher Salerno, Sarah Blake, and all the good folks at Saturnalia, past and present. Thank you family (Robert, Jean, Ryan); thank you PDX friends (Sarah Johnson, Nathan Boyer, Ingrid Kesswood): Thank you Wabash College, the Byron K. Trippet research fund, and my new colleagues in its English Department.

And, as always, my wife: Anne Fisher.

for Whit

Table of Contents

The Air

is warm with those still waiting
to be born. They flit past us

like mosquitoes, then scramble—
tenuous as the station

at the far end of the dial.
Bloodless, they're blood to us all.

By winter they lift upward
slowly, through the grainy peaks

of snowdrifts or a streetlamp's
conical glow. How small we

must seem then, how countable—
strolling home between headphones,

or desk-bound, ballpoints locked in
crosswords or 1099s.

It's only when we couple
that we too diffuse coolly,

and a voice peels from their whirl-
wind, convinced—if just briefly—

that flesh is not poured out in
small and divisible cups.

As for you—whom we address
now, though you waft through neon,

steam vents, and leaves—remember
this companionless whisper

and not our paired hands, entwined
still as we drift into sleep.

We'll both wake to so many
solitary tomorrows,

believing—if just briefly—
in a world so beautiful

that you could be assembled
from its vaporous remains.

I

The Environmentalists

Let us idle here   in this plains state's dead center.

        Let us look up—from the Quik Stop, from these gas pumps—and erase

                the landscape we've made.

Let these billboards fade till   they frame wide-open sky. Let us snuff out

the tavern signs in these two-stoplight small towns.

                      Let the antique malls fossilize and fall.

                        Let us erase it all.

We are your elegists, revealing—as we revel in—

        this radical absence.   Come sit with us, whom futility drove

           into imagination's embrace.

Let this foul scent find its path back to the feedlot;   let the sickly cows refill and fall—

their fat tails flicker like earthworms in rain.

           We forgo the chalk for the clean slate.

And you there, satisfied spectator,

        waving from the roadside we unravel   as we travel west—

      did you doubt we'd erase ourselves too?

Pages and pages   dissolve over rooftops, melting our city down to new snow.

   You were the audience we always performed for.

     We are the attar this nation distills: engines revving,

                                      our Romantic thinking,

                                      and the constant need to move on.

Behold the pastoral we've left:

     a stream thirsts inevitably lower, a groundhog

          sniffs the wind that lifts   like a bolt of snapped cloth.

   Moss grows into the crust of old porches, and you've grown

                                    into your front lawn.

How perfect is this world

    without us? It absorbs all   save we who made it this way.

Lightning 1

Were every
　　star rolled in-
to a straw

　　and snorted;
were the noon
　　sun spied through

a pinhole—
　　these all fall
shy of my

　　singular
rapture. Trust
　　in this: I

will—thrown down
　　(broken, cold)
across this

　　globe—bleach your
rods and cones.
　　We both live

in easeful
　　fleetingness.
　Don't flee it.

Litany

after the Precatio Terrae

To know what part's raw merriment, what's wrath   released

    in season—   your geysers skywrite, they loop; a mud flow moves

            every trunk and tree root. Gaia, Arbiter of the All

   Natural, we are indefatigable   readers: a cirrus cloud

        is string to tease out storms; see stones in stream—

     we pray halfway through fording.   I met a man. He sailed.

      Claimed hurricanes were coins   you clicked across your knuckle bones

   or dropped, if distracted.

        We gardeners aren't so gullible. We've watched surf toss

     a cliff's ledge like piecrust.   At whim

you'll turn your insides out—   your moods make

  my other gods a hobby.

      One day I'll relinquish weather signs

   and drift like pine needles within them.   I imagine myself

          inside both sea and sky, crashing the cheek

  of a slave girl. Diva, sweet Earth Queen—

I am an herb gatherer in search of my fair allotment.

Whatever I take from this forest floor   I borrow.

Midnight at the School of Cosmetology

and the mannequins, vacant
as Caesars in their hall of mirrors,

enthrall a night watchman.
His fingers trace their root holes'

perfect rows. This Styrofoam,
bald as the gibbous moon, outlives

the follicles of a thousand women
thinking. Last week the imported hair

shone fulgent as polygraph ink
and delicate as relics.

He still recalls its boxed arrival—
bangs, pigtails, wigs—whirlpools

of third world beauty
cut to train beauticians of tomorrow.

And though he doesn't fetishize
its climate or cuisine—pelmeni

in mayonnaise, rain sieved
from a tin roof's runoff—he's breathed

that hair before the students
kerosened it scentless.

There is a world pressed between
a harvest and its dreaming.

There is a hallway he taps his night-
stick back through, luminous

as the one he entered. All night
hairdos never to travel back overseas

dissolve in the field behind
the building. When his shift ends

he walks home and clicks the TV on.
He turns to stone till morning.

In the Shadow of a Scrivener's Quill

Over the *O*, the *ah,* the fable's lazy start, its *Once*
Upon a Time; over the gild-work and into the text block, past
the signatures and spine; over the names

remaindered from distant shores which you swept
up and re-lined; over the *we*, the *she*, the *I*; over
the cattle carts clacking on cobblestones,

dead prayers, lost plays, gun-free melees,
and the other sounds those foreign consonants retain—
over the footnotes, toward the fore edge, through

the marginalia that's raining down the vellum's white,
inviting frame; over the gaps which absent words
plant into the lines; over the cloth

that holds your place; over the ink that's dried;
over the flesh and under the hide of enough
animals it's said whole herds passed

through your hands; over the grooves
your newest word still shines inside, past the pages
bound face-to-face, revised; over the stories,

all the oldest ones, which—like light we skim
from distant stars—renders our hurtling less lonely;
over the eons, inside the authors, onto an easel

and into your inkwell, the shadow of your scrivener's quill
is dancing, dark foot dipped into a darker pool, it lifts
a load of sweet, unfiltered evening

then lands, black dash to reattach the past,
and coax us up the learning curve we climb
by generations. O monk or scribe

who curled his back inside candlelight, I've often
questioned your motives: did penitence push
you to push books into the dark beyond—

stepping stones you leapt toward St. Peter's ledger—
or was scribe work just an exercise in exercising options?
Take that candle for life's defining metaphor

and the tomes you shelve begin
to resemble heaven. Perhaps you were seduced
enough to change them, as when chaperones

left alone too long imagine misbehaving?
Or did anonymity only remind you
of the pleasures it offered in compensation: to live

for months inside Homer's head, bundled
up in one-word increments; to touch the word
of God, put it down in red, before returning

to a relay team that runs for centuries
untended? One day our world will call you up
again, place into your hands our scraps

of self, and ask you to arrange the parts
that make us sharp, redeeming. For now may you
swim inside our memory, rippling unnoticed.

The First Heartbeat

doesn't splash down,
a space capsule
            blinking its beacon
        to be found.

What warmth it bodes
derives from swarms;
            cells converge to thrum
        a rhythm.

I think of yours
and think of crowds,
            sourceless and surging
        through a cross-

walk, the footsteps
thickest beneath
            the stoplight's bleating.
        That apex

bears the largess
of everywhere
            we've traveled. You hold
        whole cities.

To dip an ear
into these notes
            then tip our heads back
        and float un-

fastened—thank you
midwife, thank you
         "fetal doppler"—melts
    us, mute now

as the novice
astronomer
         who—scoping our dark,
    cosmic start—

yearns to brush knees
with a stranger.
         Your broadcast broadens
    our tiny

kingdom. We ask,
for now, just this:
         let us never hear
    your last one.

Lightning 2

Fact: I do
    strike twice. Fact:
not one blade

    of swirling
grass can dodge
    bolts that fall

like bursting
    lightbulbs. I
plant my thoughts

    where maps aren't
yet drawn; I
    ladder down

through trees, drunks,
    and steeples.
Close your eyes.

    I preserve
what you last
    spied. Your world

is no more
    than my aft-
er image.

We Live Our Lives through Other People's Bodies

    till we're no more than campfires
our families encircle. Our families then—

beneath the lantern of a saline bag—
rehearse their own deaths through us.

Meanwhile our pores open inward
under a deluge of morphine

and memory is all we have left to eat.
Slowly it grows to enclose us, before sailing

like a whale's belly lightlessly on.

Our organs then, if we gift them to the living,
will rise, piece by piece, on cloaks

of dry ice. The small planes that await them
chirr over this city like crickets.

See their shadows leap freely, like those
of skimmed stones on the drowned.

And the men here—paused at a crosswalk
and listening—can feel their heels

lift as the crowd pushes them on.

Hide and Seek

after Matthias Sarbiewski

Our whispers stricken, glances   thinned to sheets

      the sun anneals (one ounce love yields six gilded leaves)—

           till now, my Christ,   we're separate

       as comet from constellation. My pain's enflamed

         by your infinite expansion.

    You're smoke, you're   thunder's antistatic rope, coaxing

sparks up a tree trunk.   Meanwhile, the day makes skillets from our sundials.

      Next door, the farmer harvests popcorn.   I ask him: where did

         your departure whisk you?

    The shepherd doesn't know. His trio (white flock, black   birds, black flies)

       lingers, exchanging places. A gap breaks

in a bank of clouds: your big toe testing the water?

       I ask the innkeeper, I ask

the county priest.　　　Both balance drinks upon your dog-eared book

but won't address my thirsting. Are you

　　　baked in sod, wearing

　　　whiskered moss—　　　maybe you've woven a hammock

　between the pine trees? My sweat

　　　　seeks your low ground. These sighs

　　　　travel the high plains

dodging windmills.

　　　If you're perched atop one, wait:　　I'll walk

　　　　　　beneath your sandaled feet.

My lungs are large enough to spin the blades.　　I'll glimpse you in their turning.

To Assemble This Poem Properly

    begin from above. The first line wrote itself
in eraser. Your entrance refills with its cloud.

Can you feel now a dull tug on your pant leg?
You have shadows within shadows.

The poem strips them off like spare parachutes.
Watch their dark mouths briefly glisten

like guardrail reflectors. Leave silence
between them like warm loaves of bread.

Whatever small truth the poem hurtles toward
is already in your pockets. Release it here

and stop breathing. Watch it rain down
like disco ball light. If a story comes in, cold

from the margins, you alone can warm
its feet. To do so you must hold it

beneath the voice that trails you.
You offer the one it becomes on the ground.

The seamless transfer of two people
humming is one scenario in which the poem

successfully ends. In another these couplets empty
and you are a diver climbing their cool tubes

back up to the start. From there you see its finale
clearly, but do nothing to alter its course.

You'll soon crash through a tenth story window.
Do not worry. The poem's safe.

See its thousand shards glint at your feet.

II

The Identity Thief

From you I make

a purer form of you—unencumbered by blood flow,

memory bleached clean as a set   of excavated teeth.

When creditors call you

in the evening's late hours, tell them

you've lifted airily   out of your sneakers, unspooling passwords

through phone cords and birds' hollow bones.

She's freer, she's freer, this   new self

whisked like a suit to the dry cleaner—

though I'll admit

that I slipped into her tailored sleeves.

Together we've seen   bad movies in far away cities, felt

sunrises warm our near-perfect croissants. I almost sent

you a postcard, but I found

a new lover before writing my   "Wish you were here."

Know this: I never owned anything

        more than your absence, that unspoken reassurance

       that you'll not pass

             yourself while crossing the street.

    See these faces, full now with fall's attenuated   windchill,

    each one ready for work, or sex, or sleep's long reward.

See them step   into restaurants or make way

  for their neighbors, warm in the knowledge

      that so many unknowable persons   build lives

proximate to their own.

    Now imagine that one of them shares your name.

   I am in the business   of elaborate public service.

  I robbed you of no more   than isolation's charm. We've all kept it

    in surplus, our lives equal parts

digitized and adrift.

Empathy is what I've given you, gratis.   I'll take anger in exchange for my grift.

Dementia

astounds the mind
like sunbeams shot
　　　through venetian blinds;
　　they fall in

time with the day's
slow rise. You dream
　　　this heat till the dream
　　completes you.

And we dream here
too, eight who sit
　　　and eat, each thankful
　　just to be

thinking, thinking
how far our own
　　　thoughts err or veer—what
　　did I want

at this store?—and
if you've caused our
　　　memory to cool
　　like embers.

It matters not.
Being mindful
　　　of the mind's decline
　　will not set

the dust back down
once it's gathered.
   So let us meet you
 and remeet

you where we spread
white napkins down—
   small picnic, smaller
 surrender.

You're the man who'll
see in mirrored
   glass his last, greatest
 creation.

We're the children
whom you look through
   as we try damn hard
 to feed you.

Thumbprint

Why are you sleeping   thumbs—

      Numb when I woke   up,

     Little soda thimbles? Did   you

Pass out in candle   wax

    Byproduct from writing nocturnal   poetic

      Scholarship, *Iambic Pentameter for*   *Dummies*?

My guess? You're tickling   some

     Dream girl, real no   body

    Hitchhiking Tijuana. Could you   maybe

Return by breakfast, and   cut

    The wandering? I'll drop   my

     Spoon without your opposing   nerve.

Lightning 3

Survive me
   to reveal
radiance

   in every-
thing you make
   or still are

hopelessly
   mired in.
Neckhairs swept

   like windblown
grass; bodies
   reduced to

their white-hot
   footprints? No.
I leave you

   that deeper
scar you call
   tomorrow.

The Second Year

Like the last house still lit
within a cul-de-sac

you draw the street's sporadic
light behind your glass

and hold it. Your thoughts, I mean,
they trend effortlessly inward

as less leaves you enamored.
Not long ago I scooped

a bubbled necklace
from your bath or paused

to point out—*see it, caught there
in Sutro Tower's tongs?*—the moon

still risen in the morning.
But the surprise of sidewalk stones

has given way to words;
they dull a new thing's charm,

make room for make-believe
and remembering.

I've long dreaded the latter—
how my impatience

will lodge itself inside
your mind's dark loam.

Nothing bright will thrive.
What faults of mine won't fester?

In time these words will replace
the man I'll become, while

the man I'll become
will replace the one who wrote them.

I feel your eyes upon me
endlessly. I see myself

smoldering inside them.

Glaciers

You may shrink us—we who   measured

       in inches our creep over the globe's wholeness—but not before

      we leave oceans on your front porch.

            Concision was not ours to fathom:

    how a moment—alone in the bathtub, a drop of water

   caught on an eyelash—reminds you to count

the days till another birthday.

      But now we're that droplet and the tapwater and the snowline.

    You're still confined

       inside the porcelain's frame.   Did you think our undoing

would pass by unseen? It was like   waking with no knowledge

    of evening. It was sunlight   kneading our breaddoughy backs.

   Later your drill bits

     bit us, hungry   for relics from a time you hadn't despoiled.

   We do not envy you, who delight in knowing

that you've a beginning and end.

The world thrives on contrasts—four seasons, brief lifespans—you're too keen

to dissolve.

Don't you see how you've made us

more like yourself?

So drink the water your waiter brought without asking.

Stop at the reflections we left in the Great Lakes.

Once there were plains   and merely desolate

prairies. Then a century sweated us

into our present state. We are your sustenance.   You are our bane.

Old Tyme with a *y*

When the last phone cord unslithers
from a sleeping teen's fingers,

and all the TV knobs have spun
off into orbits unknown;

when the word *tablet* can glisten
without beeswax or mason,

and I listen nightly to the mailboxes'
blue feet unbolting as they walk

empty-bellied out of town—I'll believe
then in this screen like a sleeve

my *I* slips inside to swim through an era's
rivering surge. Let its ephemera

be both my barnacles and bilge.
I can revisit my old selves at Goodwill.

And if, pausing one day in a field
of tall grass and boulders, an hour yields

its motion as if sealed under glass, I'll know
that only memory makes me whole.

To Translate This Poem Properly

      pass briskly through the door left ajar.
We thank you for your instincts.

This is not a through street, but your walking
relieves us of the need to do so

on our own. See now how silhouettes fill
the poem's many windows? Feel that glass flex

like a TV left mute. You strum the banister
till the staircase is humming. The poem

warms in the air adjoining two floors.
Its dimensions are certain; its quiets you can't touch.

And we who were the poem's former tenants
eavesdrop from a neighbor's backyard.

We authored all that unhelpful graffiti.
Our Christmas lights still stretch from the roof

to the moon. We've chased your echo
to this unremarkable crevice and will soon

trail the tongue of your tape measure home.
Let us listen now as you root

through the poem's cellar, shaking
its shoeboxes and jars. We'll meet you

in a nearby bathroom, blank as a police lineup.
Your silences leave us salivating like hounds.

Letter in a Bottle for When the Seas Rise

There was a time we knew   the seasons' tilt and turn.

    The sky told us (or those who still worked beneath   its blue) when to till;

and new TV premiered each fall.

        A storm might burst its lungs

          upon our shores, but all was cyclically foretold.

  More or less, or at least no less   than before: so we fell asleep

behind the wheel—   and drove and drove

    and drove some more,   through the snow glare of our mid-May yards.

  It covered dog and garden hose and newly sprung begonias.

    This was once upon a time,   once before we got to drinking.

Small son—

    to learn how well we've doomed the world

    will be the task we leave you;

      to learn the least you need to do   will be your children's.

  And someone—as oceans erode the shores—will learn to re-enchant it.

Meanwhile, from the crisped core

of a forest fire, we've gathered

        a bouquet of microphones to offer you   this update:

your parents have retired to a garbage flotilla,

    the one island that'll rise   above the high tide we've made.

We left binoculars in your upstairs window.

    Look at us, afloat in the whale-rich Pacific,

        reuniting with all that we've lost.

        What has the trash taught us?

That what we can't solve   will be absolved with a heartfelt goodbye.

An Ordinary Evening in San Francisco

Goodnight children my kid met at the playground.
Your pajamas wait like starfish on your small beds back home.
Goodnight street sweeper, hugging

every odd-numbered hillside. Goodnight
tomcats, marching from the Marina to the moon.
We are leaving, we are leaving, we'll not be back soon.

Tonight the lit windows only lead
to better lives and other windows. They spread
out like the cell signals shooting through this night air.

Goodnight strobing cyclist, cyclops in the near-
darkness. Goodnight bald man counting out bus fare for his son.
We are leaving, we are leaving, we'll not be back soon.

And now the last dealers disappear
into nondescript doorways; and their dead friend
drinks the cognac they left him on the curb.

We carry this evening to a back booth
at Tosca; we drink Irish coffee and sketch out bus routes,
long as tablecloths, to anywhere we'd call home.

The bartender sees himself in the table he's wiping
but still hasn't noticed that we've stolen his miniature spoon.
We are leaving, we are leaving, we'll not be back soon.

We leave and start walking. We say goodnight
to the smartphones swimming upstream like salmon.
Goodnight umbrellas, jostling for your six feet of dry air.

We crowd into a BART car that breathes underwater
and feel our eardrums dissolve. My son sees this crush
of bodies as a chance to try counting. We tell him

we are leaving, we are leaving, we'll not be back soon.

Mary of Egypt

[Her historicity remains uncertain. A sixth-century *vita* identifies her as a Judean singer. A half-century later she is a nun with no name. The following narrative, based on Sophronios (ca. 560 – 638), finds her as a prostitute who, struck by a holy vision, abandons Jerusalem for the desert. Forty-six years later she tells her story to Zosimas, a passing monk.]

Colloquy with St. Mary of Egypt

1.

The oldest of the Old World roils—   that desert, dear,

        of your redemption. Do cheers, tear gas, or wails

    move you, sleepless still, through

            streets you once abandoned?   In bookstacks, yes,

      we met   unmoored from our centuries.

A man whom I made speak had made you speak

      till we three fled   that tattered crime scene.

              And now in frescoed Lent, in hagiographic glass

2.

I seek you: unfed & thinly androgynous—

        a cloak to ward off cold

    and loathsome nakedness, your hand   receding, silvery as our moonlit surf—

     or so the Byzantines once painted.

      Does your halo hail me   or receive true believers?

    However its gold foil glows, know

       this: that grandeur's only possible with pressure.

Sainthood encircles you.   The stoplight shifts to yellow.

3.

And people—stacked day long   upon other people—intersperse

      prematurely. It is evening, mid-November,   MUNI crowds

        merge and mull, spilling out from sidewalks.

  And there's steam and glances

held two beats too long   and the taqueria's lime-sweet ventilation.

     Though we live out dense, almost-island lives

    our appetites narrow the space between us.   I walk

      into this rush-hour crush   and wait for it

4.

to move me.   I long to lead you

through this throb and throng—   past tram wires & the Transamerica spire,

    past taillights

 on fog-locked hillsides.   We're flush with light not warmth.

  We take sex as winter's savior.

    Do you feel it—vaguely waiting, willfully bated—in these jostled bodies?

  Fucking here holds such small,   semantic thrall; clothing

whispers free in the mind's undressing.   This Mission, this city

5.

saintly named, teems with so many

I see as you,   a girl—she glances back, she ambles on—

reminds me why neck tattoos   are sexy:

we want our pictures *whole*; we must imagine her   unshirted to do so.

Young still, loving a lovely wife

and son,   I turn toward home, kiss your gilded hand, and think

this icon's flatness

does not suit you.

6.

Wilderness, a few trunks upthrust

and zero underbrush, no berries   or thirst-quenching streams—

that is all I expected.

Penitent first, only later saint, I walk this dirt

I'm meant (with my three meager

loaves) to love   as one might their ancestral acreage.

And I too borrowed tongues to succumb—

what lover doesn't know   lovers everywhere are actors?

7.

Mary—   I am a man transfixed by you

but fixed into (forgive this thought) his home's   small lot:

I picture winters thinner, whole years

lost like toys beneath couch pillows.

And yet this city's bodies move

aware of their own bodies.   I feel them, lithe in denim, a wind

with hips I'd press into or kill for.   I feel them but must come home

to wife and son—   lest your story

8.

detain me. Those who've tell it call you harlot, pray to a hermit—

forgetting how both roles hold

such freedom: I watch a woman's hand ascend a thigh;

I stare into a window where someone reads past midnight.

I am only free

in the day's in-betweens, eavesdropping on outdoor bars

or lifting into the lives   uncurtained above them—

Mary, take my hand and deliver me   into either, into ether.

9.

How many voices, various timbres,

        possessed me   until (46 years gone) I barely owned my own?

       With Zosimas I summoned everyone

I'd ever heard to muster my own story.   Beside his muse, the monk could not move.

          Speech is heat

      emanating from a body, strengthened by the pores that warm it—

            the mouth is only its holiest exit.

    I am weary here, upon your lips: your nearness exceeds your reverence.

10.

So let me hover over yours—

      hands cupped above a potter's wheel—I'll palm

    your warmth, or shape it.   Fall brings Dungeness crab and stone fruit.

The streetlamps must last a little longer.

      And we two, who shall lie mild, linger together

in restaurant corners

    where the rich leave wine unfinished.   I drink; you drink—

         There must be more than words

11.

between us.   So here's a story: there was a man

                              who so loved an ancient tongue that he felt

        a millenium of air   collapse

    in loamy pronunciations. He'd blush and brim

                with a wantonness that could—when translated—consume him.

        Once, snowbound in Louisville, he did nothing else.

            For days he hoarded syllables

                        as one would the stars in heaven.

12.

But now his house stirs

                        with its own small voice, sweet as a mockingbird

        or echo. What joy to hear   his words turned back

on him; what fear   to know his discontent is mimicked.

A smart friend (ok, my therapist) advised: "To change the way

        you see the world remember: your kid still sees his world   through you."

Teach me   how to want less, or want me.

Give me your wilderness, or will me to refuse it.

13.

I am altogether earth and ash and flesh,

Alexandrian by birth—a runaway who resorted   to sorting flaxseed.

                    I asked for alms. I asked to be neither wife nor daughter.

          Then, waking one afternoon, I saw a lover leave me

  coin, oblivious to that rarer gift

                                        he'd offered: he *listened.*

                September followed, the Exaltation of the Holy Cross,

and pilgrims bathing by the seaside.   My body—warm as the unraked sand—

14.

          bought me safe passage.

                              All toward Jerusalem the sea lurched—boat, man, and me

          rocking unsteadily. My shamelessness was such I drank

the world up through their hungry bodies.   Why did the sea

          not swallow us whole, drown our unholy journey?

                              On land I found new hands, a mob which—

driven by love of one—offered   the pleasure

                                        of being pressed by many.

15.

Is that dark, understated charge why you dawdle

now, one more domestic truant?　　　　　Here's where it led me:

　　　　　Up till dawn, waiting on church gates　　　　　to swing free,

　　　　　I was three times　　　　　denied entry.

I held tight to the holiest I found;

　　　　　I watched a groping couple going forward. Still, I sat there

　　still—　　anchored to that courtyard's refuse.

　　　　　It was then that She appeared　　　and then the desert.

16.

So meet me where the grass is cool and lovers—scarved

　in darkness—hide their mischief.　　Here is Mission Dolores Park: dusklight, caressing.

　　　　　Its namesake welcomes

　worshippers one block north. Each group seeks

　　　　　　　　　a voice that will embrace it.

　　　　　Both will trade in secrets.

So let us drift through this potsmoked playground.

I am more real　　than the priests I meet　　who only love you for converting.

17.

Lights aswirl around my head

        and the refrain of lascivious songs—

    my three loaves gone   to stone, and errant weeds I'd suck the juice from:

these were my first 17 years. Such is the solitude (thirst

    then lust compounding thirst) you swoon for?

One whole month I refused the sky,   my tears

    feeding the desert. At its close I lacked both food and clothes.

      My name never felt so good   as when *I* yelled it skyward.

18.

And She (gentler now, voice   faint as a fruit bat

gauging the distance to its dugout) gave reply—

          and I'd no longer want for meal,

          embracing rock when shelter was unforthcoming.

I was happy then, unbidden;

     my refusals rained down

  from a beetle's whirring wingtips.

    I'll call you love, my love,   when you feed on the Word alone, as given.

19.

Praise be then to thee   who lives in sumptuous destitution.

       Is this blasphemy? (So be it.) Tragedy (one poet said) is

               imagination showing us lives we can't access.   But you

    refuse it all; I wish heaven

                     was more than the belabored words

      meant to preserve me. How would you, Mary, have me

         proffer myself more?   I'll disengage (through penitence

         or praise of you) from this erotic world,   but you are all my fancy.

20.

I walk to Mission and Cesar Chavez.

I stand beneath St. Luke's—of her holiness, Sutter Health; of the angels

who cut a son from my love—and remember   our pediatric doc

               who told us this story about honey:

Once upon a time three soldiers wandered through the desert.

One stumbled into a hole. It oozed with honey.

      And then they dug   to find the head, immaculate, that it surrounded.

    And then they ate till morning.   Dear Mary, I would dip—

21.

—into the sweetness I'm embalmed in?

My boy (whose night-long psalm the dark

has, piecemeal, discharged, whose hunger—cold   as an unstruck bell—

still rules him) you sweeten

me too, ummortify my appetites—   or are at least persistent.

Put my name

upon your tongue. (*It's done.*) Divest yourself   of all that's not

its sound (*the honey, the sun*) then repeat it till

22.

the Virgin fills you—   I will be there too, much

freer, a mouth   where you presupposed an entrance.

Or linger on this secret:

I've imagined—in Lent's fifth Saturday, in a *vita* penned and passed and read again—heaven held

in unborn vocal chords,

life's desultory remnant (*may one reader*

retain us).   You're discontent with contentedness?

I've loved

23.

        Zosimas since he entered

   a fantasy the desert cold had gilded.   He squinted, light glinting

       off the gypsum.   How long did I hold there, unclothed, before

    I took the cloak he offered?

Its flesh and fur encircled me   but asked for nothing.

He heard everything you've heard.

You owe your hearing it to his words, rivering down through others' words,

   each younger than the last one.   I only asked a year (*tell me why*) before his retelling.

24.

Because I was indebted to Her   who'd quarantined the world;

because Zosimas pledged a future communion;

because his eyes distilled

       the sky

            and I'd grown accustomed to watch where I was walking;

because I could lodge myself—   a pebble or peppercorn—

beneath his tongue

        and he'd return me to his monastery in secret.

25.

And so you went unuttered.

Mary, this much this city's taught me:

                              sex is the earth's endless pull; it exerts

            itself regardless   of the bodies that will or won't receive you.

        Likewise words, which don't just preserve, but *weigh*—

                    their grief is in their gravity, and names

                build out their own exacting orbit.   By the way,

                                        you can call me Derek.

26.

Love, allow me my refusals.

I could remain Hers till heard as his.   To undim my name

                    would mean one thing: Zosimas could not return it.

His cloak became the vellum

                                    sheaves I couldn't read

but knew his musk passed through: I rubbed the hide that withstood the world.

                I smelled the flesh that felt his lungs' upheavel.

                    Come: approach *this* page and breathe

27.

till your lover fills your dormant senses—

                that was my summer, fall, and winter.

Zosimas returned beneath a moon full as a silver coin,   and I walked

                          upon the Jordan to greet him.

      He brought figs & sweet legumes. A chalice

held our Lord's blood, though it was that blood's messenger   I followed.

          Desire, you say,

            moves you now?   It is dissimilitude that will save you.

28.

I would hide   in the love you hid

from Zosimas, or loft myself   into those altitudes that still nuture solitude—

      I'd move like a dandelion's white thread

   through flight patterns   headed home; I'd drift past lovers sipping

            sodas below their baggage.   But no.

                  I can hold here half a night or more,

another figure in fog, fastidious   and lonely,

      but it's better to wrestle a compromise from two truths

29.

and call it a conclusion.

       "I love you," the semiotician tells his love.

       "I love you," he repeats, but also means: "I need to hang up the phone."

          Is marriage not equally a metaphor—   resigned to reconciling

                                                contradictions?

      I hold my mouth, Mary, beneath this stream, knowing

          my baptism cannot catch you.   I make of you a mask

only to find myself   tricked into communion.

30.

It is blood and it is wine.

And Zosimas—who alone beheld my full self—

      returned home, blind to the sinner   he'd resurrected.

      Only then did sand seem like a page   untarnished. And I who couldn't read

         was writing: "Dear Father—

    bury this body, a humble Mary, in red

desert's morn. Here reborn, I will   to *dust* this *dust*

    return—   For me, Lord, shall Zosimas pray.   He'll be here, a year's time.

31.

    In the month of Pharmouthi (so say the Egyptians)

    In the month of April (so say the Romans)

  on the Passion's last night

    died I. My Last Supper, Zosimas gave—"   and I gave him my flesh to bury.

This, my friend, was where my speech   was meant to end: sand

    warmed by sun, ants inside my letters' grooves, darkly glowing.

  But *you* had to escape   on the lips

  of your creation.   We all wear masks, my love, to make it through the evening.

32.

Our love then, forever ours:

           whatever darkness splits us.

        Today I read that Voyager had shook free from our sun

and soared—interstellar orphan—on a course

    that home star charted.   Whatever children, whatever lovers,

      bid us elsewhere, our signal lingers

             blinking, blushing—

red as the pulse beneath your sunburn.

33.

I run my fingers along a building's brickwork.

I feel the shoulders (cool in T-shirts, maybe strapless) on which the mortar pressed

     its pattern. I feel the shirts unbutton—

                          and it is nothing.

     I shall instead bear down—

bear you, Mary, down to basement stacks, and then bear home;

     let whispers lead you down,   let my paleness pass now

    like a moon sailing beyond your window.

34.

The street is bright with constellated smartphones—

          and sparks of trolley wire, and foreclosed storefronts—and I am

   led on   now by what's left of you, my Northstar

        in shattered stained glass. I scatter you like the coins

    that made music in my pocket.

       And yet, and yet   my jawbone aches

        that you, unbeknownst to most   (or soon to be),

        might irrevocably   kiss me.

35.

Dear boy: We've touched   and touched   and touched

     in the space between these lines—   your lips are ever more

          upon my lips: what is imitation

    but a love   ground so fine you breathe it in unknowing?

    All my pores release   themselves to ruin or rain.

       You delight in me, dream me silky thoughts   you'd surrender to—

but when have you thought to have me?

Mine's a body you would (like Zosimas) obscure   but never enter.

36.

    I lay you down in the crowd boarding the 14L.   Find an expression here

        that suits you. Let these people lead you

      home; let this city   spin its nocturnal charm or turn

        into a ball of foreign words—   a gift

to offer your son   and one your wife's already given.

    Listen now: her syllables (я тебя) are palatalized air (люблю)   and diaphragm,

  tapwater (мой мальчик)   and (мой сын) farmers' market produce—

        Your voices rise from bookmarks.

37.

Mary of Egypt, Mistress Mary, Mary My Ascetic   whose name is the lone weight

I carry from this evening: when it tolls, this charm I stole, for saviors,

        singers, gardens—

        let it toll always as thee.   Behold: I take this bell of you

        before you sail off unbodied.

I pass through MUNI's pneumatic doors, past sputtering cars, and see three men

        asleep in St. Mary's Park, off Crescent.

Return to your lion's grave   smoother than mortuary stone

38.

        as I return home and crack the door to hear—

        in words she learned one by goddamn one; in a voice

other than the voice we love in—   my wife sing our small son down.

And he is singing there beside her.

    I sip her honeyed tea till a hive   hums inside me.

    Rain forks against the glass, and I fold

        my old words into Zosimas and Talbot and Sophronios.

    Sleep now—   we are the shroud you shine through.

Heliotrope, Or
Man's Mind Angles Inevitably Toward God

after Jacob Balde

No sliver of self   held in reserve, no

       life left but the one untangled from a sun ray.

     I am a builder of footstools, crates.   I am countless nods

       begun in the direction of my last benediction.

My servitude must be verbally attested:

     I vow

         to rake His heat into a Libyan beach; to let waves wash glass curtains.

         I vow to cut Carpathian surf with oars on loan from Homer.

     No jackknifed raft, no   cormorant (lured

         to me by the moon's dead eye) will delay

my time inside His stain-glassed iris.

       The sins I've long messengered   He'll release

as if speeding through a flipbook.

My friends,

the North Pole's just one half of this archer's crosshairs.

His quiver is limitless.

All seek its acupuncture.

See them shuffle up and stand. Their shadows follow like regimental backup.

They count

their wounds to four and fall away.

The rest kneel or bow.

We smaller targets prove Him the finer marksman.

Notes

The Environmentalists": See Alan Weisman's *The World Without Us* (2007).

"Litany," "Hide and Seek," and "Heliotrope, Or Man's Mind Angles Inevitably Toward God" are all adaptations from minor or Neo-Latin poems, modeled on Lowell's *Imitations* (1961), wherein "one voice run[s] through many personalities, contrasts and repetitions."

"Dementia" is for H. Max Murray (1922 – 2011).

"Colloquy with St. Mary of Egypt"

1.6   "A man whom I made speak": Jacob Balde (1604 – 1668), an Alsatian Jesuit and Neo-Latin poet. Once, while serenading his lover from beneath her window, he overheard singing in a chapel next door. The next day, it's said, he converted.

6.1-8   An interjection, however brief. Also a rebuttal.

9.1-8   She returns, but won't begin her story in full until 13.1.

11.7   "hoarded syllables": Latin, with its quantitative prosody, lends itself to mouthy, self-satisfying utterance. Sophronios wrote in Greek.

16.1-8   The poet, progressing south, becomes insistent, interruptive.

19 – 20   The inkling of a dialogue. She will anticipate him in 21.1.

19.1   "sumptuous destitution": Richard Wilbur's phrase for Dickinson.

19.2   "Tragedy (one poet said)": the poet is T.S. Eliot.

20.1-4   "of the angels / who cut a son": The poet—out of self-pity, out of exhaustion—said the following as he put on his scrubs: "I feel like I'm headed into Chernobyl." The obstetrician's reply: "Uh uh, honey. You've already been through that. This here's the easy part."

21.7   "(*It's done*)": Bolder, more welcome, he is able now to slip answers into her sentence.

22.4   "Lent's fifth Saturday": John Berryman, this poem's silent patron, reminds us that the date can coincide with April 1st ("April Fool's Day, or, St Mary of Egypt," *The Dream Songs* 47).

26.4   "vellum": calfskin treated for use in early manuscripts. The finest variety was *uterine*, pages made "from the skins of unborn or stillborn animals" (*The Bookman's Glossary*).

27.5-8   Her coyness extends into the afterlife. Sophronios writes of them reciting the Lord's prayer, and when "the prayer [had] come to an end, according to custom she gave the monk the kiss of love on his mouth" (trans. Maria Kouli).

29.2-3   "I need to hang up": Barthes's point here relates (unsurprisingly) to both semiotics and eros. The phone bit is courtesy of Ira Glass (*This American Life*, episode 514).

31.4   "I gave him my flesh": Zosimas "ran up to her and bathed the feet of the blessed woman with his tears, for he did not dare to touch any other part" (Sophronios). A lion dug the grave.

33.6   "basement stacks": a composite, by now, of Doane Library (Denison University), Rackham Graduate Library (University of Michigan), and Stanford's Green.

35 – 36   Her final reassurance, lodged in the poem's coda. The poet returns in full by 37.1.

36.6-7   "Я тебя люблю, мой мальчик, мой сын": Russian, "I love you, my little boy, my son."

37.7   "St. Mary's Park, off Crescent": conveniently, coincidentally, a three block walk from his home in the neighborhood of Bernal Heights.

38.7   "Talbot and Sophronios": see *Holy Women of Byzantium: Ten Saints' Lives in English Translation* (1996), edited by Alice-Mary Talbot. Also of use: *The Life of St. Mary of Egypt* (1974), edited and translated by Mother Katherine and Mother Thekla.

Previous Winners of the Saturnalia Books Poetry Prize:

Soft Volcano by Libby Burton

Telepathologies by Cortney Lamar Charleston

Ritual & Bit by Robert Ostrom

Neighbors by Jay Nebel

Thieves in the Afterlife by Kendra DeColo

Lullaby (with Exit Sign) by Hadara Bar-Nadav

My Scarlet Ways by Tanya Larkin

The Little Office of the Immaculate Conception by Martha Silano

Personification by Margaret Ronda

To the Bone by Sebastian Agudelo

Famous Last Words by Catherine Pierce

Dummy Fire by Sarah Vap

Correspondence by Kathleen Graber

The Babies by Sabrina Orah Mark

Also Available from saturnalia books:

For Hunger by Margaret Ronda

Live at the Bitter End by Ed Pavlic

I Think I'm Ready to See Frank Ocean by Shayla Lawson

The New Nudity by Hadara Bar-Nadav

The Bosses by Sebastian Agudelo

Sweet Insurgent by Elyse Fenton

The True Book of Animal Homes by Allison Titus

Plucking the Stinger by Stephanie Rogers

The Tornado Is the World by Catherine Pierce

Steal It Back by Sandra Simonds

In Memory of Brilliance and Value by Michael Robins

Industry of Brief Distraction by Laurie Saurborn Young

That Our Eyes Be Rigged by Kristi Maxwell

Don't Go Back to Sleep by Timothy Liu

Reckless Lovely by Martha Silano

A spell of songs by Peter Jay Shippy

Each Chartered Street by Sebastian Agudelo

No Object by Natalie Shapero

Nowhere Fast by William Kulik

Arco Iris by Sarah Vap

The Girls of Peculiar by Catherine Pierce

Xing by Debora Kuan

Other Romes by Derek Mong

Faulkner's Rosary by Sarah Vap

Tsim Tsum by Sabrina Orah Mark

Hush Sessions by Kristi Maxwell

Days of Unwilling by Cal Bedient

Gurlesque: the new grrly, grotesque, burlesque poetics edited by Lara Glenum and Arielle Greenberg

Letters to Poets: Conversations about Poetics, Politics, and Community edited by Jennifer Firestone and Dana Teen Lomax

Artist/Poet Collaboration Series:

Velleity's Shade by Star Black / Artwork by Bill Knott

Polytheogamy by Timothy Liu / Artwork by Greg Drasler

Midnights by Jane Miller / Artwork by Beverly Pepper

Stigmata Errata Etcetera by Bill Knott / Artwork by Star Black

Ing Grish by John Yau / Artwork by Thomas Nozkowski

Blackboards by Tomaz Salamun / Artwork by Metka Krasovec